The Wonder of Comfort

Books edited by Phyllis Hobe
Published by The Westminster Press

The Wonder of Comfort
The Wonder of Love
The Wonder of Prayer

The Wonder of Comfort

Edited by
Phyllis Hobe

*Drawings by
Jennifer Cole*

**Bridgebooks
Philadelphia**

Copyright © 1982 Phyllis Hobe

Book Design by Alice Derr

First edition

Bridgebooks
Published by The Westminster Press®
Philadelphia, Pennsylvania

PRINTED IN THE UNITED STATES OF AMERICA
9 8 7 6 5 4 3 2 1

Library of Congress Cataloging in Publication Data

Main entry under title:

The Wonder of comfort.

Includes indexes.
1. Consolation—Quotations, maxims, etc. I. Hobe,
Phyllis.
BV4905.2.W66 1982   242   82-8322
ISBN 0-664-26003-9   AACR2

Contents

Acknowledgments

"Meet the Master," by Charles L. Allen. From *The Charles L. Allen Treasury*, by Charles L. Allen, copyright © 1970 by Fleming H. Revell Company. Used by permission.

"To One in Sorrow," from *Songs of Hope*, by Grace Noll Crowell. Copyright 1938 by Harper & Row, Publishers, Inc.; renewed 1966 by Grace Noll Crowell. Reprinted by permission of the publisher.

"Individuality" and "Happiness Comes," from *Because I Love You*, by Alice Joyce Davidson. Copyright © 1982 by Alice Joyce Davidson. Published by Fleming H. Revell Company. Used by permission.

"The Family Table," by Marjorie Holmes, originally appeared in *American Home*, copyright © 1961 by The Curtis Publishing Company. From the book *Love and Laughter*, by Marjorie Holmes. Reprinted by permission of Doubleday & Company, Inc.

The poems of Helen Steiner Rice are reprinted by permission of Gibson Greeting Cards, Inc., Cincinnati, Ohio 45237.

Three excerpts from *In the Vineyard of the Lord*, by Helen Steiner Rice, copyright © 1979 by Helen Steiner Rice and Fred Bauer. Published by Fleming H. Revell Company. Used by permission.

Diligent effort has been made to locate and secure permission for the inclusion of all copyrighted material in this book. If any such acknowledgments have been inadvertently omitted, or if such were not received by the time of publication, the editor and publisher would appreciate receiving full information so that proper credit may be given in future editions.

Introduction

by Eugenia Price

I have a dear friend who can stand looking at a tree or a greening spring vine in silent, awe-filled *wonder* for a longer time than most of us can endure silence. Such moments contain, perhaps, the best definition of the word *wonder*. Most of us overuse the word to such an extent that it loses its meaning. I have observed that my friend seldom speaks of anything being "wonderful." She has entered into the word and understands its uniqueness.

To wonder is not a commonplace—except as are sunsets, the many greens of early summer, sunrises, tide rhythms, and other dependable gifts of God. Do we grow careless in our use of the word because we can depend upon God giving us seasons, tides, and the coming and going of days?

Beside me as I write is the small, potent treasury called THE WONDER OF COMFORT. An impending sorrow in my own life has opened a door for me to grasp—not as a commonplace, but as a thing of awe—the short, readable, carefully made selections which Phyllis Hobe has found in a way I might not normally feel a need to do. Comfort is here for anyone in need of it. No one is immune to tragedy, to grief, to daily irritations. Everyone at one time or another cries out to be comforted. Prepare yourself to find comfort in these pages and to wonder at it.

Our God *is* the God of all comfort. One short line in this book was put there, I am convinced, just for me in my current need: "God is awake." Your line is undoubtedly here, too. THE WONDER OF COMFORT is not for reading and discarding. It is to be kept and wondered over.

I. Faith

"... Trust in the Lord ..."
Proverbs 3:5

TRUST

Oh, face to face with trouble,
    Friend, I have often stood,
To learn that pain hath sweetness,
    To know that God is good.
Arise and meet the daylight,
    Be strong and do your best,
With an honest heart and a childlike trust
    That God will do the rest.

Margaret E. Sangster

In the eyes of God, we all are children, and Jesus is our teacher. If anything, the parent has more to learn from the child, because one of the first things Jesus teaches us is that, in order to understand the things of God, we must become childlike. If we can do that, then when he holds out his hand, we will grasp it in complete trust. Where he leads us, we will follow, not as a somber duty but as a joyful adventure.

Colleen Townsend Evans

When a man surveys his past from middle age he must surely ask himself what those bygone years have taught him. If I have learned anything in the swift unrolling of the web of time, it is the virtue of tolerance, of moderation in thought and deed, of forbearance toward one's fellowmen.

I have come also to acknowledge the great illusion which lies in the pursuit of a purely material goal. What slight satisfaction lies in temporal honor and worldly grandeur! All the material possessions for which I strove so strenuously mean less to me now than a glance of love from those who are dear to me.

Above all am I convinced of the need, irrevocable and inescapable, of every human heart, for God. No matter how we try to escape, to lose ourselves in restless seeking, we cannot separate ourselves from our divine source. There is no substitute for God.

A. J. Cronin

Yourself in your own hands is a problem and a pain; yourself in the hands of God is a possibility and a power.

E. Stanley Jones

Sometimes I consider myself
there as a stone before a carver,
whereof he is to make a statue;
presenting myself thus before
God, I desire Him to form His
perfect image in my soul, and
make me entirely like Himself.

Brother Lawrence

TO CLOSE THE DAY

The day, with the work God gave me to do, is done,
and now He has given me the night, quiet and soothing,
for rest. I will, therefore, trust myself—body and spirit—into His loving, tender care, through the mystery of
sleep. As flood tides from the ocean fill each bay or inlet,
so power and love and peace can fill my life to overflowing as I rest quietly, serenely, patiently, bravely, lovingly,
with confidence and perfect faith.

Author unknown

God knoweth best what is need-
ful for us, and all that He does is
for our good.

Brother Lawrence

I ONLY KNOW HE DID

I stood beneath a mighty oak
  And wondered at its size,
How from an acorn it could grow
  I never could surmise—
  I only know it did.

How God could make the heavens,
  The water and the land,
The animals and vegetables,
  I cannot understand—
  I only know He did.

I do not know how God could come
  And cleanse my heart from sin
Through Jesus Christ, His blessed Son,
  Whose life abides within—
  I only know He did.

Author unknown

In the bonds of Death He lay
  Who for our offence was slain;
But the Lord is risen to-day,
  Christ hath brought us life again,
Wherefore let us all rejoice,
Singing loud, with cheerful voice,
  Hallelujah!

Martin Luther

He brought light out of darkness, not out of a lesser light; he can bring thy summer out of winter, though thou have no spring; though in the ways of fortune or understanding or conscience, thou have been benighted till now, wintered and frozen, clouded and eclipsed, damped and benumbed, smothered and stupefied till now, now God comes to thee, not as in the dawning of the day, not as in the bud of the spring, but as the sun at noon.

John Donne

LEARNED TO TRUST

I have no answer for myself or thee,
Save that I learned beside my mother's knee:
"All is of God that is, and is to be;
And God is good." Let this suffice us still,
Resting in childlike trust upon His will
Who moves to His great ends unthwarted by the ill.

William Cowper

Have courage for the great sorrows of life and patience for the small ones; and when you have laboriously accomplished your daily task, go to sleep in peace. God is awake.

Victor Hugo

17

I have held many things in my hands, and have lost them all; but whatever I have placed in God's hands, that I still possess.

Martin Luther

"Keep this for me."
What child has not said this,
And placed a treasure in his Mother's hand
With strict injunction she should keep it safe
Till he return?
He knows with her it will be safe;
No troubled thought or anxious fear besets his mind,
And off he runs light-hearted to his play.

If children can so trust, why cannot we,
And place our treasures, too, in God's safe hand;
Our hopes, ambitions, needs, and those we love,
Just see them, in his all-embracing care,
And say with joyous heart, "They are with Thee."

Author unknown

Trust in the Lord with all thine heart; and lean not unto thine own understanding.

In all thy ways acknowledge him, and he shall direct thy paths.

Proverbs 3:5–6

I can do all things through Christ which strengtheneth me.

Philippians 4:13

TRUST

Build a little fence of trust
  Around today;
Fill each space with loving work
  And therein stay;
Look not through the sheltering bars
  Upon tomorrow,
God will help thee bear what comes,
  Of joy or sorrow.

Mary Frances Butts

There is a divinity that shapes our ends,
Rough-hew them how we will.

William Shakespeare

Do everything for God, uniting yourself to Him by a mere upward glance, or by the overflowing of your heart towards Him. Never be in a hurry. . . . Do not lose your inward peace for anything whatsoever, even if your whole world seems upset. Commend all to God, and then lie still and be at rest. . . . Whatever happens, abide steadfast in a determination to cling simply to God, trusting to His eternal love for you; and if you find that you have wandered forth from this shelter, recall your heart quietly and simply.

Francis de Sales

THE MYSTERIOUS WAY

God moves in a mysterious way
  His wonders to perform;
He plants His footsteps in the sea
  And rides upon the storm.

Deep in unfathomable mines
  Of never-failing skill,
He treasures up His bright designs
  And works His sovereign will.

Ye fearful saints, fresh courage take:
  The clouds ye so much dread
Are big with mercy, and shall break
  In blessings on your head.

Judge not the Lord by feeble sense,
  But trust Him for His grace;
Behind a frowning providence
  He hides a smiling face.

His purposes will ripen fast,
  Unfolding every hour;
The bud may have a bitter taste,
  But sweet will be the flower.

Blind unbelief is sure to err,
  And scan His work in vain;
God is His own interpreter,
  And He will make it plain.

William Cowper

No soul can be forever banned,
Eternally bereft:
Whoever falls from God's right hand
is caught into his left.

Edwin Markham

SHUT IN

Shut in? Ah, yes, that's so,
As far as getting out may go,
Shut in away from earthly cares,
But not shut out from Him who cares.

Shut in from many a futile quest,
But Christ can be your daily Guest.
He's not shut out by your four walls,
But hears and answers all your calls.

Shut in with God, oh that should be
Such a wonderful opportunity.
Then after you have done your best,
In God's hands safely leave the rest.

Author unknown

OUT IN THE FIELDS WITH GOD

The little cares that fretted me,
   I lost them yesterday,
Among the fields above the sea,
   Among the winds at play,
Among the lowing of the herds,
   The rustling of the trees,
Among the singing of the birds,
   The humming of the bees.

The foolish fears of what might pass
   I cast them all away
Among the clover-scented grass
   Among the new-mown hay,
Among the rustling of the corn
   Where drowsy poppies nod,
Where ill thoughts die and good are born—
   Out in the fields with God!

Author unknown

II. Kindness

"... If I can stop one heart
from breaking ..."

Emily Dickinson

THANK GOD FOR LITTLE THINGS

Thank you, God, for little things
   that often come our way,
The things we take for granted
   but don't mention when we pray,
The unexpected courtesy,
   the thoughtful, kindly deed,
A hand reached out to help us
   in the time of sudden need—
Oh make us more aware, dear God,
   of little daily graces
That come to us with "sweet surprise"
   from never-dreamed-of places.

Helen Steiner Rice

Doing good to others is not a
duty. It is a joy, for it increases
your own health and happiness.

Zoroaster

He who allows a day to pass without practicing generosity or enjoying life's pleasure is like a blacksmith's bellows—he breathes but does not live.

Lowell Thomas

THE GIFT OF FRIENDS

God knew we needed something more
Than budding earth and sunlit sky,
And so He sent us friends to love,
To lift our hearts and spirits high;
God chose to teach Love's wondrous art,
Of comfort, cheer that never ends
By giving to the thankful heart
The dear, good gift of faithful friends.

Author unknown

Each time we meet, you always say
    Some word of praise that makes me gay.
You see some hidden, struggling trait,
    Encourage it and make it great.
Tight-fisted little buds of good
    Bloom large because you said they would.
A glad, mad music in me sings;
    My soul sprouts tiny flaming wings.
My day takes on a brand-new zest.
    Your gift of praising brings my best,
Revives my spirit, flings it high;
    For God loves praise, and so do I.

Author unknown

If I can stop one heart from breaking,
I shall not live in vain;
If I can ease one life the aching,
Or cool one pain,
Or help one fainting robin
Unto his nest again,
I shall not live in vain.

Emily Dickinson

THINGS THAT NEVER DIE

The pure, the bright, the beautiful,
　　That stirred our hearts in youth,
The impulses to wordless prayer,
　　The dreams of love and truth;
The longings after something lost,
　　The spirit's yearning cry,
The strivings after better hopes—
　　These things can never die.

The timid hand stretched forth to aid
　　A brother in his need,
A kindly word in grief's dark hour
　　That proves a friend indeed;
The plea for mercy softly breathed,
　　When justice threatens nigh,
The sorrow of a contrite heart—
　　These things shall never die.

The cruel and bitter word,
  That wounded as it fell;
The chilling want of sympathy
  We feel, but never tell;
The hard repulse that chills the heart,
  Whose hopes were bounding high,
In an unfading record kept—
  These things shall never die.

Let nothing pass, for every hand
  Must find some work to do;
Lose not a chance to waken love—
  Be firm, and just, and true:
So shall a light that cannot fade
  Beam on thee from on high,
And angel voices say to thee—
  These things shall never die.

Charles Dickens

Speak gently: it is better far
  To rule by love than fear;
Speak gently: let not harsh words mar
  The good we might do here.

Speak gently: love doth whisper low
  The vows that true hearts bind;
And gently friendship's accents flow:
  Affection's voice is kind.

Speak gently to the little child;
  Its love be sure to gain;
Teach it in accents soft and mild:
  It may not long remain.

Speak gently to the aged one;
  Grieve not the careworn heart;
The sands of life are nearly run:
  Let such in peace depart.

Speak gently to the young; for they
  Will have enough to bear;
Pass through this life as best they may,
  'Tis full of anxious care.

Speak gently, kindly, to the poor;
  Let no harsh tones be heard:
They have enough they must endure,
  Without an unkind word.

Speak gently to the erring; know
  They may have toiled in vain;
Perchance unkindness made them so:
  Oh, win them back again.

Speak gently: He who gave his life
  To bend man's stubborn will,
When elements were in fierce strife,
  Said to them, "Peace, be still!"

Speak gently: 'tis a little thing
  Dropp'd in the heart's deep well;
The good, the joy, which it may bring
  Eternity shall tell.

Lewis J. Bates

INDIVIDUALITY

All of us are blessed with
Individuality,
We're different from each other—
That's how God meant us to be,
So when opinions differ,
And you don't see eye to eye,
Or angry words are spoken
And tempers start to fly,
Calm yourself and try to see
The other person's view—
Mediate your differences
As God wants you to do,
For by living well with others
Through every kind of strife,
Our horizons broaden
And we get much more from life!

Alice Joyce Davidson

Great occasions for serving God
come seldom, but little ones surround us daily.

Francis de Sales

III. Serenity

"... to be at peace with myself ..."
Anne Morrow Lindbergh

THANK GOD

Thank God for dawn,
The songs of birds,
Awakening earth,
And browsing herds.

Thank God for work
And well-filled day,
For power to serve
The joyous way.

Thank God for friends
And fireside talks,
Inspiring books,
And pleasant walks.

Thank God for night
And Silence deep,
Protecting Love,
And peaceful Sleep.

Grenville Kleiser

I want first of all . . . to be at peace with myself. I want a singleness of eye, a purity of intention, a central core to my life. . . . I want, in fact—to borrow from the language of the saints—to live "in grace" as much of the time as possible.

Anne Morrow Lindbergh

THE PENDULUM

There was once a pendulum waiting to be fixed on a new clock. It began to calculate how long it would be before the big wheels were worn out and its work was done. It would be expected to tick night and day, so many times a minute, sixty times that every hour, and twenty-four times that every day and three hundred and sixty-five times that every year. It was awful! Quite a row of figures, enough to stagger you! Millions of ticks! "I can never do it," said the poor pendulum. But the clockmaster encouraged it. "You can do one tick at a time?" he said. "Oh, yes," the pendulum could do that. "Well," he said, "that is all that will be required of you." So the pendulum went to work, steadily ticking, one tick at a time, and it is ticking yet, quite cheerfully.

Dwight Lyman Moody

Why should we be in such
desperate haste to succeed
and in such desperate enterprises?
If a man does not keep pace
with his companions,
perhaps it is because he hears
a different drummer.
Let him step to the music
he hears,
however measured or far away.

Henry David Thoreau

The important thing is to know
how to take all things quietly.

Michael Faraday

I am an old man and have
known a great many troubles, but
most of them never happened.

Mark Twain

ODE ON SOLITUDE

Happy the man whose wish and care
  A few paternal acres bound,
Content to breathe his native air
  In his own ground.

Whose herd with milk, whose fields with bread,
  Whose flocks supply him with attire,
Whose trees in summer yield him shade,
  In winter fire.

Alexander Pope

Whatsoever things are true,
Whatsoever things are honest,
Whatsoever things are just,
Whatsoever things are pure,
Whatsoever things are lovely,
Whatsoever things are of good report;

If there be any virtue,
and if there be any praise,
think on these things.

Philippians 4:8

Quiet minds can not be per-
plexed or frightened, but go on in
fortune or misfortune at their own
private pace, like a clock during a
thunderstorm.

Robert Louis Stevenson

DECALOGUE

I. Never put off till tomorrow what you can do
today.
II. Never trouble another for what you can do
yourself.
III. Never spend your money before you have it.
IV. Never buy what you do not want, because it is
cheap; it will be dear to you.
V. Pride costs us more than hunger, thirst, and
cold.
VI. We never repent of having eaten too little.
VII. Nothing is troublesome that we do willingly.
VIII. How much pain have cost us the evils which
have never happened.
IX. Take things always by their smooth handle.
X. When angry, count ten, before you speak; if
very angry, an hundred.

Thomas Jefferson

WALKING WITH GOD

O for a closer walk with God,
  A calm and heavenly frame,
A light to shine upon the road
  That leads me to the Lamb!

Where is the blessedness I knew
  When first I saw the Lord?
Where is the soul-refreshing view
  Of Jesus and His word?

What peaceful hours I once enjoy'd!
  How sweet their memory still!
But they have left an aching void,
  The world can never fill.

Return, O holy Dove, return,
  Sweet messenger of rest:
I hate the sins that made Thee mourn,
  And drove Thee from my breast.

The dearest idol I have known,
  Whate'er that idol be,
Help me to tear it from Thy throne,
  And worship only Thee.

So shall my walk be close with God,
  Calm and serene my frame;
So purer light shall mark the road
  That leads me to the Lamb.

William Cowper

If the vessel of our soul is still tossed with winds and storms, let us awake the Lord, who reposes in it, and He will quickly calm the sea.

Brother Lawrence

Twice happy is she
content with her task,
Who still keeps her
vision beyond.

Sarah K. Smith

Do the very best you can and leave the outcome to God.

Author unknown

Never a tear bedims the eye
That time and patience will not dry.

Bret Harte

Give us grace and strength to persevere. Give us courage and gaiety and the quiet mind. Spare to us our friends and soften to us our enemies.

Robert Louis Stevenson

For all your days prepare,
　And meet them ever alike:
When you are the anvil, bear—
　When you are the hammer, strike.

Edwin Markham

WHEN THE STARS ARE GONE

The stars shine over the mountains,
　the stars shine over the sea,
The stars look up to the mighty God,
　the stars look down on me;
The stars shall last for a million years,
　a million years and a day,
But God and I will live and love
　when the stars have passed away.

Robert Louis Stevenson

AWARENESS

To live content with small means.

To seek elegance rather than luxury,
    and refinement rather than fashion.

To be worthy, not respectable,
    and wealthy, not rich.

To study hard, think quietly,
    talk gently, act frankly.

To listen to stars and birds,
    to babes and sages, with open heart.

To bear all cheerfully, do all bravely,
    await occasion, hurry never.

In a word, to let the spiritual,
    unbidden and unconscious, grow up
    through the common.

    This is to be my symphony.

William Ellery Channing

There is a serene and settled
majesty to woodland scenery that
enters into the soul and delights
and elevates it, and fills it with
noble inclinations.

Washington Irving

SONG

When I am dead, my dearest,
  Sing no sad songs for me;
Plant thou no roses at my head,
  Nor shady cypress tree:
Be the green grass above me
  With showers and dewdrops wet;
And if thou wilt, remember,
  And if thou wilt, forget.

I shall not see the shadows,
  I shall not feel the rain;
I shall not hear the nightingale
  Sing on, as if in pain;
And dreaming through the twilight
  That doth not rise nor set,
Haply I may remember,
  And haply may forget.

Christina Rossetti

A thing of beauty is a joy forever:
Its loveliness increases; it will never
Pass into nothingness; but still will keep
A bower quiet for us, and a sleep
Full of sweet dreams, and health,
    and quiet breathing.

John Keats

THE BOOK MORE PRECIOUS THAN GOLD

Though the cover is worn,
And the pages are torn,
  And though places bear traces of tears,
Yet more precious than gold
Is the Book worn and old,
  That can shatter and scatter my fears.

When I prayerfully look
In the precious old Book,
  As my eyes scan the pages I see
Many tokens of love
From the Father above,
  Who is nearest and dearest to me.

This old Book is my guide,
'Tis a friend by my side,
  It will lighten and brighten my way;
And each promise I find
Soothes and gladdens my mind
  As I read it and heed it today.

Author unknown

Day is done, gone the sun
From the lake, from the hills, from the sky.
Safely rest, all is well! God is nigh.

Author unknown

Lose who may—I still can say,
Those who win heaven, blest are they!

Robert Browning

THE BIBLE

We search the world for truth. We cull
The good, the true, the beautiful,
From graven stone and written scroll,
And all old flower-fields of the soul;
And, weary seekers of the best,
We come back laden from our quest,
To find that all the sages said
Is in the Book our mothers read.

John Greenleaf Whittier

From "PIPPA PASSES"

The year's at the spring
And day's at the morn;
Morning's at seven:
The hillside's dew-pearled;
The lark's on the wing;
The snail's on the thorn;
God's in his heaven—
All's right with the world!

Robert Browning

IV. Consolation

"... The Shepherd was there ..."
Dale Evans Rogers

A DOUBLE DOSE OF COURAGE

It startled me at first!
Yet by a mountain stream
I saw a blind man painting
A golden sunset scene.
At first I stood amazed,
Yet one with fingers gone
Was strumming his guitar
And humming low a song.
It seemed incredible!
Yet one who lost her child
Stood up in praise of God
And through her tears she smiled.
"Impossible," I said.
Yet sipping sorrow's cup
I saw a widow go
To cheer her neighbors up.
I doubted it at first,
Yet going to his store
My wheelchair neighbor smiled
Each day he passed my door.
How grand that God pours out
On those crushed down with sadness
A double dose of courage,
An extra cup of gladness.

Perry Tanksley

God uses broken things. It takes broken soil to produce a crop, broken clouds to give rain, broken grain to give bread, broken bread to give strength. It is the broken alabaster box that gives forth perfume. . . . It is Peter, weeping bitterly, who returns to greater power than ever.

Vance Havner

I WISH YOU

I wish you
some new love
of lovely things,
and some new forgetfulness
of the teasing things,
and some higher pride
in the praising things,
and some sweeter peace
from the hurrying things,
and some closer fence
from the worrying things.

John Ruskin

ABRAHAM LINCOLN'S LETTER
TO COLONEL ELLSWORTH'S PARENTS

Washington, D.C., May 25, 1861

My Dear Sir and Madam:

In the untimely loss of your noble son, our affliction here is scarcely less than your own. So much of promised usefulness to one's country, and of bright hopes for one's self and friends, have rarely been so suddenly dashed as in his fall. In size, in years, and in youthful appearance a boy only, his power to command men was surpassingly great. This power, combined with a fine intellect, an indomitable energy, and a taste altogether military, constituted in him, as seemed to me, the best natural talent in that department I ever knew.

And yet he was singularly modest and deferential in social intercourse. My acquaintance with him began less than two years ago; yet through the latter half of the intervening period it was as intimate as the disparity of our ages and my engrossing engagements would permit. To me he appeared to have no indulgences or pastimes; and I never heard him utter a profane or intemperate word. What was conclusive of his good heart, he never forgot his parents. The honors he labored for so laudably, and for which in the sad end he so gallantly gave his life, he meant for them no less than for himself.

In the hope that it may be no intrusion upon the sacredness of your sorrow, I have ventured to address you this tribute to the memory of my young friend and your brave and early fallen child.

May God give you that consolation which is beyond all earthly power.

Abraham Lincoln

Recently I have been going through many hours of soul searching and walking through dark times that come to us all. But I know God is behind the "dark cloud" that engulfs me, and I must endure it until He removes the darkness, for this is not a destructive experience but a constructive one. I am sure He is trying to awaken me to a new awareness of how to best serve Him. And after my old self dies completely, I will have moved a little closer to God.

Helen Steiner Rice

TO ONE IN SORROW

Let me come in where you are weeping, friend,
And let me take your hand.
I, who have known a sorrow such as yours,
Can understand.
Let me come in—I would be very still
Beside you in your grief;
I would not bid you cease your weeping, friend,
Tears bring relief.
Let me come in—I would only breathe a prayer,
And hold your hand,
For I have known a sorrow such as yours,
And understand.

Grace Noll Crowell

LIFE'S LESSON

There are times in one's life when all the world seems to turn against us. Our motives are misunderstood, our words misconstrued, an unkind word reveals to us the unfriendly feelings of others.

The fact is, that it is rare when injustice, or slights, patiently borne, do not leave the heart at the close of the day filled with a marvelous sense of peace—perhaps not at once—but after you've had a chance to reflect a bit. It is the seed God has sown, springing up and bearing fruit.

We learn, as the years roll onward and we leave the past behind, that much we had counted sorrow, but proved that God is kind; that many a flower we'd longed for had hidden a thorn of pain, and many a rugged by-path led to fields of ripened grain.

The clouds that cover the sunshine; they cannot banish the sun. And the earth shines out the brighter when the weary rain is done. We must stand in the deepest shadow to see the clearest light; and often through Wrong's own darkness comes the welcome strength of Right.

Ella Wheeler Wilcox

Be not grieved above measure for thy deceased friends. They are not dead, but have only finished the journey which is necessary for every one of us to take. We ourselves must go to that great place of reception in which they are all of them assembled, and in this general rendezvous of mankind, live together in another state of being.

Antiphanes

The world is so empty if one thinks only of mountains, rivers, and cities; but to know someone who thinks and feels with us, and who, though distant, is close to us in spirit, this makes the earth for us an inhabited garden.

Johann Wolfgang von Goethe

Oh, the comfort, the inexpressible comfort of feeling safe with a person; having neither to weigh thoughts nor measure words, but to pour them all out, just as they are, chaff and grain together, knowing that a faithful hand will take and sift them, keep what is worth keeping, and then, with the breath of kindness, blow the rest away.

George Eliot

But open your eyes and the world is full of God.

Jacob Boehme

OUR BURDEN BEARER

The little sharp vexations
    And the briars that cut the feet,
Why not take all to the Helper
    Who has never failed us yet?
Tell Him about the heartache,
    And tell Him the longings too,
Tell Him the baffled purpose
    When we scarce know what to do.
Then, leaving all our weakness
    With the One divinely strong,
Forget that we bore the burden
    And carry away the song.

Phillips Brooks

Some people go around underestimating their great potential. You are a very special person, and you should thank God every day that you have a keen, sensitive, and perceptive mind. God has made you a beautiful, warm, wonderful individual.

Helen Steiner Rice

O God of love, who art in all places and times, pour the balm of thy comfort upon every lonely heart. Have pity upon those who are bereft of human love, and on those to whom it has never come. Be unto them a strong consolation, and in the end give them fullness of joy, for the sake of Jesus Christ, thy Son, our Lord.

Anonymous

The amen of Nature is always a flower.

Oliver Wendell Holmes

SUNRISE

Though the midnight found us weary,
    The morning brings us cheer;
Thank God for every sunrise
    In the circuit of the year.

Margaret E. Sangster

SOMEBODY LOVES YOU

SOMEBODY LOVES YOU more than you know,
SOMEBODY GOES WITH YOU wherever you go,
SOMEBODY REALLY and TRULY CARES
And LOVINGLY LISTENS TO ALL OF YOUR
  PRAYERS . . .
Don't doubt for a minute
  that this is not true,
For GOD loves HIS CHILDREN
  and takes care of them, too. . . .
And all of HIS TREASURES
  are yours to share
If you love HIM completely
  and show HIM you care . . .
And if you "WALK IN HIS FOOTSTEPS"
  and have the FAITH to BELIEVE,
There's nothing you ask for
  that you will not receive!

Helen Steiner Rice

THE SHEPHERD WAS THERE

Even when I have been forced to walk in the valley of the shadow of death, I have learned not to be afraid. When our little girl died in 1952, the Lord showed me that He was there in the valley with me and that He had the whole situation well in hand, and asked only that I trust Him. Little Robin was unconscious most of the day she died. There were two nurses with her, and I was in and out of her room all day. She had encephalitis—brain fever—a complication which developed from mumps. Our doctor told us at noon that she was terribly ill and might not make it. I walked outside and a soft breeze fanned my face. I seemed to be in another world, and God was there. At four o'clock in the afternoon I went into the kitchen to prepare supper for the other children, and while I was doing it I suddenly knew that the Lord was going to take Robin home. I said aloud, "It's all right, Lord. She's Yours." Mind you I adored this baby, and for two years I had fought to keep her alive.

At 7:45 I went in and kissed her good-by. Her breathing was labored. I turned and walked across the room: Lana, the big gray dog who loved Robin, was scratching furiously at the screen door and barking excitedly. Do dogs have a sense of approaching death? I know many people who believe they do. I walked down to the barn, praying and asking the Shepherd, "Please don't let her suffer any more. Please take her quickly." As I came back to the house Virginia, one of her nurses, met me and said quietly, "She's gone, Dale." Roy and I

60

had a hard short cry, and then—peace. There seemed to be Someone Else with us. . . .

All through the next two days, all through the day of the funeral, the Shepherd was there. I had the feeling that Robin was there too, *that somehow it was all right,* and that it was best for all of us. The Shepherd never left us in the valley. I could never have walked through it without Him.

Dale Evans Rogers

THOU ART NEAR

O Love Divine, that stooped to share
   Our deepest pang, our bitterest tear,
On Thee we cast each earth-born care,
   We smile at pain while Thou art near.

Though long the weary way we tread,
   And sorrow crown each lingering year,
No path we shun, no darkness dread,
   Our heart still whispering "Thou art near."

Oliver Wendell Holmes

V. Joy of Life

"... Today is the time
to be happy ..."

Lawrence Hawthorne

HAPPINESS COMES

God laughs
in sunbeams

golden sunbeams
of love
of hope
of faith

and when
His golden sunbeams
dance upon
your heart

happiness comes.

Alice Joyce Davidson

Life is a mirror: if you frown at
it, it frowns back; if you smile, it
returns the greeting.

William Thackeray

Half the joy of life is in little things taken on the run. Let us run if we must—even the sands do that—but let us keep our hearts young and our eyes open that nothing worth our while shall escape us.

Victor Cherbuliez

The best things are nearest: breath in your nostrils, light in your eyes, flowers at your feet, duties at your hand, the path of Right just before you. Then do not grasp at the stars, but do life's plain, common work as it comes, certain that daily duties and daily bread are the sweetest things of life.

Robert Louis Stevenson

There's music in the sighing of a reed;
There's music in the gushing of a rill;
There's music in all things, if man had ears:
The earth is but the music of the sphere.

Lord Byron

A SMILE

Nothing on earth can smile but man! Gems may flash reflected light, but what is a diamond-flash compared to an eye-flash and a mirth-flash? Flowers cannot smile; this is a charm that even they cannot claim. It is the prerogative of man; it is the color which love wears, and cheerfulness, and joy—these three. It is a light in the windows of the face, by which the heart signifies it is at home and waiting. A face that cannot smile is like a bud that cannot blossom, and dries up on the stalk. Laughter is day, and sobriety is night, and a smile is the twilight that hovers gently between both—more bewitching than either.

Henry Ward Beecher

THE THOUGHT OF BEAUTY

A choir boy's voice, a ship in sail, an opening flower, a town at night, the song of the blackbird, a lovely poem, leaf shadows, a child's grace, the starry skies, a cathedral, apple trees in spring, a thoroughbred horse, sheepbells on a hill, a rippling stream, a butterfly, the crescent moon—the thousand sights or sounds or words that evoke in us the thought of beauty—these are the drops of rain that keep the human spirit from death by drought. They are a soothing and a silent refreshment that we perhaps do not think about but which goes on all the time.

John Galsworthy

THE FAMILY TABLE

You sit around it together, the antique black walnut table that your husband bought with a bunch of junk furniture and lovingly refinished years ago.

It took him months to complete that single project, so carefully did he sand and plane and varnish and wax, until its surface was smooth as glass and hard as stone. It will take the hottest dish and survive the roughest blows. The dog has chewed its legs without much damage; it wasn't too much hurt even when chafing dish caught fire once and burned up a tablecloth. Long and steady it stands there, opening up for additional leaves when guests are coming, shrinking smaller and smaller as children go away from home.

How many meals have been served there? you sometimes wonder, getting down the plates to set it another time. How many birthday cakes and Thanksgiving turkeys and Christmas dinners has it known? How many kites have littered its broad expanse, how many model planes and scrapbooks and doll clothes?

How many bills have been paid there, how many notes written to teachers, how many income tax forms? For that matter, how many apples have probably been peeled there, how much canning done? For it bore the marks of knives and jars and water buckets when your husband first came carting it home.

And you think back to all those other lives which came to this selfsame table before you. The women, busy at their humble kitchen tasks before clearing it, as was often done, to set it for supper. The men who sat down to carve. And the children, the many children, excited about their birthday cakes, their Thanksgiving drumsticks, their news about love affairs or school.

People. Living people drawn together at a sturdy table. And you think of the laughter and the tears and the arguments and stormy scenes this table has known. They are its essence, a part of it like its grain. And it is this which gives an antique its true value and meaning. It is old and warm and wise with living. It is like a person who only grows more beautiful with age.

Marjorie Holmes

JOY OF LIFE

The joy of life is living it and doing things of worth,
In making bright and fruitful all the barren spots
    of earth.
In facing odds and mastering them and rising
    from defeat,
And making true what once was false,
    and what was bitter, sweet.
For only he knows perfect joy whose little bit of soil
Is richer ground than what it was when he began to toil.

Author unknown

BARTER

Life has loveliness to sell,
   All beautiful and splendid things,
Blue waves whitened on a cliff,
   Soaring fire that sways and sings,
And children's faces looking up
Holding wonder like a cup.

Life has loveliness to sell,
   Music like a curve of gold,
Scent of pine trees in the rain,
   Eyes that love you, arms that hold,
And for your spirit's still delight,
Holy thoughts that star the night.

Spend all you have for loveliness,
   Buy it and never count the cost;
For one white singing hour of peace
   Count many a year of strife well lost,
And for a breath of ecstasy
Give all you have been, or could be.

Sara Teasdale

If wrinkles must be written
upon our brows, let them not be
written upon the heart. The spirit
should not grow old.

James A. Garfield

To me, old age is always fifteen years older than I am.

Bernard Baruch

To be seventy years young is sometimes far more cheerful and hopeful than to be forty years old.

Oliver Wendell Holmes

From "GOD'S WORLD"

Lord, I do fear
Thou'st made the world too beautiful this year.
My soul is all but out of me—let fall
No burning leaf; prithee, let no bird call.

Edna St. Vincent Millay

The longer I live the more my mind dwells upon the beauty and the wonder of the world.

John Burroughs

BEAUTY OF LIFE

Beauty of life has been given to me
In the patterned leaf of every tree;
In the golden gleam of each ray of light
That comes to me from morn till night;
In the radiant color of every flower,
In fashioned garden or country bower;
In the lilting music of wood bird's call,
In the voice of a dear one, best of all.

Beauty for eye and ear and hand,
In voice of sea and voice of land;
Roaring of waves with a rhythmic din,
A low refrain from a violin;
Touch of the hand of a dear old friend,
Words of kindness without end;
Love of man and woman and child
Of all God's creatures tame and wild.

Love of the life that was given to me,
Love of life that is to be;
Love of my work and its stern command,
Love of the strength that is in my hand;
O beauty of life that has come to me,
Let me be grateful enought for thee;
Let me live on and say alway,
"Thank God for the beauty I've found today."

Mary Miles Colrin

RICHER TODAY

You are richer today than you were yesterday . . . if you have laughed often, given something, forgiven even more, made a new friend today, or made stepping-stones of stumbling-blocks; if you have thought more in terms of "thyself" than of "myself," or if you have succeeded in being cheerful even if you were weary. You are richer tonight than you were this morning . . . if you have taken time to trace the handiwork of God in the commonplace things of life, or if you have learned to count out things that really do not count, or if you have been a little blinder to the faults of friend or foe. You are richer if a little child has smiled at you, and a stray dog has licked your hand, or if you have looked for the best in others, and have given others the best in you.

Anonymous

Happiness is as a butterfly, which, when pursued, is always just beyond your grasp, but which, if you will sit down quietly, may alight upon you.

Happiness in this world, when it comes, comes incidentally. Make it the object of pursuit, and it leads us a wild-goose chase, and is never attained.

Nathaniel Hawthorne

TODAY

A young man lives in the future;
  An old man lives in the past.
For youth, time is moving too slowly;
  For age, it is moving too fast.

A young man dreams of the gladness
  The years just before him will bring;
An old man dreams of his pleasures
  When life held the wonder of spring.

But youth and age are in error!
  The present alone can convey
The joy and cheer and contentment
  We seek as we journey life's way.

Today is the time to be happy!
  No matter how young or how old,
It's always today that must bring us
  The blessings our fortunes unfold!

Lawrence Hawthorne

MORNING

Those of us who work for our living may complain about having to get up early in the morning. That's human nature, to complain about something because we do not recognize it for the blessing it is.

"What?" you may cry. "Having to get up early in the morning is a blessing?"

It may be a blessing in disguise, but it is a blessing nonetheless. Morning is a time of calm and beauty, and one of God's special treats for His favorite people.

His favorite people, of course, are those who face His days eagerly.

To be sure, morning is no treat for someone who has gone to bed too late, or for someone who fills his mornings with dread and hurry and reluctance, as so many do. Many people start the day resenting that they have duties, cursing their expulsion from the womb of sleep, and then go off to work without looking right or left, as if their own lethargy gave them tunnel-vision.

On the other hand, there is the person who has taught himself to appreciate morning and its promises. Listen, for example, to the hymn that Daniel Webster sang to morning:

"I know the morning—I am acquainted with it, and I love it. I love it fresh and sweet as it is—a daily new creation, breaking forth and calling all that have life and breath and being to a new adoration, new enjoyments, and new gratitude."

Author unknown

THINKING HAPPINESS

Think of the things that make you happy,
  Not the things that make you sad;
Think of the fine and true in mankind,
  Not its sordid side and bad;
Think of the blessings that surround you,
  Not the ones that are denied;
Think of the virtues of your friendships,
  Not the weak and faulty side;

Think of the gains you've made in business,
  Not the losses you've incurred;
Think of the good of you that's spoken,
  Not some cruel, hostile word;
Think of the days of health and pleasure,
  Not the days of woe and pain;
Think of the days alive with sunshine,
  Not the dismal days of rain;

Think of the hopes that lie before you,
  Not the waste that lies behind;
Think of the treasures you have gathered,
  Not the ones you've failed to find;
Think of the service you may render,
  Not of serving self alone;
Think of the happiness of others,
  And in this you'll find your own!

Robert E. Farley

VI. Hope

"... I know that God is good ..."
John Greenleaf Whittier

I know that God is the Answer to everything. I do not believe anything ever dies, for in the Kingdom of the Lord there is nothing lost forever—not a grain of sand, not a drop of rain, not a crystal of dew. So why should we ever think that God would create man to end in nothingness? I solve my problems one by one, asking nothing of tomorrow—only God's will be done.

Helen Steiner Rice

Who walks the world with soul awake
    Finds beauty everywhere;
Though labor be his portion,
    Though sorrow be his share,
He looks beyond obscuring clouds,
    Sure that the light is there!

Florence Earle Coates

God shall be my hope, . . .
My stay, my guide and lantern
to my feet.

William Shakespeare

From "THE ETERNAL GOODNESS"

I see the wrong that round me lies,
    I feel the guilt within;
I hear, with groan and travail-cries,
    The world confess its sin.

Yet, in the maddening maze of things,
    And tossed by storm and flood,
To one fixed trust my spirit clings;
    I know that God is good!

I long for household voices gone,
    For vanished smiles I long,
But God hath led my dear ones on,
    And He can do no wrong.

I know not what the future hath
    Of marvel or surprise,
Assured alone that life and death
    His mercy underlies.

John Greenleaf Whittier

FATHER, HOW WIDE
THY GLORIES SHINE

Father, how wide thy glories shine,
God of the universe, and mine!
Thy goodness watches o'er the whole,
As all mankind were but one soul,
Yet keeps my every sacred hair,
As I remain'd thy single care.

Charles Wesley

BE STRONG!

Be strong!
We are not here to play, to dream, to drift;
We have hard work to do and loads to lift;
Shun not the struggle—face it; 'tis God's gift.

Be strong!
Say not, "The days are evil. Who's to blame?"
And fold the hands and acquiesce—oh, shame!
Stand up, speak out, and bravely, in God's name.

Be strong!
It matters not how deep intrenched the wrong,
How hard the battle goes, the day how long;
Faint not—fight on! Tomorrow comes the song.

Maltbie D. Babcock

Just over the hill is a beautiful
valley, but you must climb the hill
to see it.

Author unknown

I am going your way, so let us go
hand in hand.

William Morris

VICTORY IN DEFEAT

Defeat may serve as well as victory
　　To shake the soul and let the glory out.
When the great oak is straining in the wind,
　　The boughs drink in new beauty, and the trunk
Sends down a deeper root on the windward side.
　　Only the soul that knows the mighty grief
Can know the mighty rapture. Sorrows come
　　To stretch out spaces in the heart for joy.

Edwin Markham

There is something good in all weathers. If it doesn't happen to be good for my work today, it's good for some other man's today, and will come around for me tomorrow.

Charles Dickens

Walk on a rainbow trail; walk on a trail of song, and all about you will be beauty. There is a way out of every dark mist, over a rainbow trail.

Navajo song

I NEVER SAW A MOOR

I never saw a moor,
I never saw the sea;
Yet know I how the heather looks,
And what a wave must be.

I never spoke with God,
Nor visited in Heaven;
Yet certain am I of the spot
As if the chart were given.

Emily Dickinson

Discouragement is always from beneath; encouragement is always from above.

Amy Carmichael

All creatures that have wings can escape from every snare that is set for them if only they will fly high enough; and the soul that uses its wings can always find a sure "way to escape" from all that can hurt or trouble it.

What, then, are these wings? Their secret is contained in the words, "They that wait upon the Lord." The soul that waits upon the Lord is the soul that is entirely surrendered to Him, and that trusts Him perfectly. Therefore we might name our wings the wings of Surrender and of Trust. I mean by this, that if we will only surrender ourselves utterly to the Lord, and will trust Him perfectly, we shall find our souls "Mounting up with wings as eagles" to the "heavenly places" in Christ Jesus, where earthly annoyances or sorrows have no power to disturb us.

Hannah Whitall Smith

FAITH

Faith came singing into my room,
  And other guests took flight;
Fear and anxiety, grief and gloom
  Sped out into the night.
I wondered that such peace could be,
  But Faith said gently, "Don't you see?
They really cannot live with me."

Author unknown

Tomorrow is a new day; begin it well and serenely and with too high a spirit to be cumbered with your old nonsense.

Ralph Waldo Emerson

Far away there in the sunshine are my highest aspirations. I may not reach them, but I can look up and see their beauty, believe in them, and try to follow where they lead.

Louisa May Alcott

When things go wrong as they sometimes will,
When the road you're trudging seems all uphill,
When the funds are low and the debts are high,
And you want to smile, but you have to sigh,

When care is pressing you down a bit,
Rest if you must, but don't you quit.
Life is queer with its twists and turns,
As every one of us sometimes learns,
And many a failure turns about
When he might have won had he stuck it out.
Don't give up though the pace seems slow—
You may succeed with another blow!

Success is failure turned inside out—
The silver tint of the clouds of doubt,
And you never can tell just how close you are,
It may be near when it seems so far.
So stick to the fight when you're hardest hit—
It's when things seem worst that you must not quit.

Author unknown

Over the winter glaciers
I see the summer glow,
And through the wide-piled snowdrift
The warm rosebuds below.

Ralph Waldo Emerson

AFTER THE WINTER . . .
GOD SENDS THE SPRING

Springtime is a season
  Of Hope and Joy and Cheer,
There's beauty all around us
  To see and touch and hear . . .
So, no matter how downhearted
  And discouraged we may be,
New Hope is born when we behold
  Leaves budding on a tree . . .
Or when we see a timid flower
  Push through the frozen sod
And open wide in glad surprise
  Its petaled eyes to God . . .
For this is just God saying—
  "Lift up your eyes to Me,
And the bleakness of your spirit,
  Like the budding springtime tree,
Will lose its wintry darkness
  And your heavy heart will sing"—
For God never sends The Winter
  Without the Joy of Spring.

Helen Steiner Rice

In the hour of adversity be not without hope
For crystal rain falls from black clouds.

Nizami

THE FOUNTAIN

Into the sunshine,
  Full of the light,
Leaping and flashing
  Morning and night;

Into the moonlight,
  Whiter than snow,
Waving so flower-like
  When the winds blow;

Into the starlight
  Rushing in spray,
Happy at midnight,
  Happy by day;

Even in motion,
  Blithesome and cheery,
Still climbing heavenward,
  Never aweary;

Glorious fountain,
  Let my heart be
Fresh, changeful, constant,
  Upward, like thee!

James Russell Lowell

WHEN DO WE GROW OLD?

Nobody grows old merely by living a number of years. People grow old by deserting their ideals. Years may wrinkle the skin, but to give up interest wrinkles the soul. Worry, doubt, self-distrust, fear, and despair— these are the long, long years that bow the head and turn the growing spirit back to dust.

Whatever your years, there is in every being's heart the love of wonder, the undaunted challenge of events, the unfailing childlike appetite for what is next, and the joy and the game of life. You are as young as your faith, as old as your doubt; as young as your self-confidence, as old as your fear; as young as your hope, as old as your despair. In the central place of every heart there is a recording chamber; so long as it receives messages of beauty, cheer, and courage, so long are you young.

When the wires are all down and your heart is covered with the snows of pessimism and the ice of cynicism, then, and then only, are you grown old.

General Douglas A. MacArthur

As for old age, embrace and love it. It abounds with pleasure if you know how to use it. The gradually declining years are among the sweetest in a man's life; and I maintain that even when they have reached the extreme limit, they have their pleasure still.

Seneca

Grow old along with me!
   The best is yet to be,
The last of life, for which the first was made:
   Our times are in his hand
   Who saith "A whole I planned,
Youth shows but half; trust God:
   see all, nor be afraid!"

Robert Browning

HOME AT LAST

To an open house in the evening,
Home shall men come,
To an older place than Eden,
And a taller town than Rome.
To the end of the way of the wandering star,
To the things that cannot be and are,
To the place where God was homeless,
And all men are at home.

Gilbert Keith Chesterton

Our Creator would never have made such lovely days, and have given us the deep hearts to enjoy them, above and beyond all thought, unless we were meant to be immortal.

Nathaniel Hawthorne

There is a land of pure delight,
Where saints immortal reign;
Infinite day excludes the night,
And pleasures banish pain.

Isaac Watts

EXAMPLE

Like the star
Shining afar
Slowly now
And without rest,
Let each man turn, with steady sway,
Round the task that rules the day
And do his best.

Johann Wolfgang von Goethe

EACH SPRING,
GOD RENEWS HIS PROMISE

Long, long ago
   in a land far away,
There came the dawn
   of the first Easter Day,
And each year we see
   that promise reborn
That God gave the world
   on that first Easter Morn . . .
For in each waking flower
   And each singing bird,
The PROMISE of Easter
   is witnessed and heard,
And Spring is God's way
   of speaking to men
And renewing the promise
   of Easter again,
For death is a season
   that man must pass through
And, just like the flowers,
   God wakens him, too . . .
So why should we grieve
   when our loved ones die,
For we'll meet them again
   in a "cloudless sky"—
For Easter is more
   than a beautiful story,
It's the promise of life
   and ETERNAL GLORY.

Helen Steiner Rice

I will lift up mine eyes unto the hills,
　　from whence cometh my help.
My help cometh from the Lord,
　　which made heaven and earth.
He will not suffer thy foot to be moved:
　　he that keepeth thee will not slumber.
Behold, he that keepeth Israel
　　shall neither slumber nor sleep.
The Lord is thy keeper:
　　the Lord is thy shade
　　　　upon thy right hand.
The sun shall not smite thee by day,
　　nor the moon by night.
The Lord shall preserve thee from all evil:
　　he shall preserve thy soul.
The Lord shall preserve thy going out
　　and thy coming in
　　　　from this time forth, and even for evermore.

Psalm 121

MEET THE MASTER

He was born in a village, of poor parents, in an insignificant little country. When He was twelve years old He was conscious of the fact that God had placed Him here for a specific purpose. At the age of thirty He made public His plans and purposes and began the three short years of His public ministry.

He loved people and enjoyed being with them. He went to their parties; He was a popular dinner guest; even the little children crowded around Him. He invited twelve men to work with Him, and later He commissioned them to carry on His work. He told a ruler about an experience called the "new birth."

He offered an outcast woman water that would quench the thirst of her very soul. He healed the sick, raised the dead, opened the eyes of the blind, loosed the tongues of the dumb, brought hearing to the deaf, and caused the lame to walk. He fed those who were hungry, and brought peace to troubled minds.

He taught the people that happiness comes from the inside, that the solution to hates and prejudices is not in laws but in love. He told of the amazing power of prayer, that the treasures one lays up in heaven are more important than the treasures one accumulates on earth, that a divided heart leads to destruction.

Faith in God was to Him a matter of supreme importance. Because God so beautifully clothed the lilies of the field, and because God cared so tenderly for even the birds of the air, He concluded that humans who are to live eternally should not worry about the things of this life. Instead, one should seek God's Kingdom first and the other things of life would be taken care of.

He warned against people judging each other. He warned that a life built on any other principles than the ones He taught would be like a house built on sand that would not stand in the face of a storm.

He said that His Kingdom was like the growth of the tiny seed that eventually becomes a tree, or like the leaven that eventually leavens the entire loaf. And that possessing Him was worth all else one had, just as the merchant sold all his possessions in order to own the one pearl of supreme worth.

When one of His disciples suggested, after a marvelous worship experience, that He just continue there, He refused. Every mountain-top experience of worship was translated by Him into acts of service and of living. He said that the way to become great was to become a servant.

Firmly He taught that one is never justified in holding an unforgiving spirit. To a crowd which was preparing to stone a sinner to death He suggested that the one without sin cast the first stone. And to the sinner He said, "Neither do I condemn thee, go and sin no more." He loved sinners and freely forgave everyone who would accept forgiveness.

Simple stories from every day life illustrated the eternal principles He taught. The Samaritan who turned aside to help one in need, the foolish shepherd who hunted until he found just one lost sheep, the father who welcomed his prodigal son home, are some of those stories.

He wept with friends who had lost a loved one by death. He was disappointed when some people He had healed expressed no gratitude. He pointed out that God expects every person to do his part, even though he has only one talent.

He cursed a fig tree for not producing fruit. He drove people out of the church who were misusing it. He said that we have duties to our government and duties to God. He praised a widow who gave a small gift.

He did not want to die, but He chose death rather than lower His standards. But as He died He prayed for the forgiveness of those who were killing Him, He gave comfort to a man dying with Him, He thought of the care of His mother, and He expressed His faith in God.

Three days after He was buried, He came back to life. He spoke to a woman. He encouraged some disheartened people, He spoke peace to His disciples, and one morning He even cooked their breakfast. He told His few followers to carry on His work until it covers the world, and finally He ascended into heaven.

He is today the one hope of the world. He is Jesus Christ, the Son of God and the Saviour of man.

Charles L. Allen

When you yourself have begun to be a new person,
      then there
is hope for your own problem whatever it is—hope for a
solution to the strained relations in your office
hope for a better understanding and a discovery
      of a new love
for your husband or wife, a new spirit in your home
      and a
happiness you had thought was gone forever
hope for a new meaning to your life
      and a new reason for
living hope . . . hope . . . hope.
Don't give up.
There's still hope.

Peter Marshall

Index of Authors

Index of Titles

Index of First Lines